101 THINGS YOU CAN DO WITH A BOOGER

By: Han Kerchief
Illustrator: David Wilcove

@Copyright 2015 by Douglas R. Eagen

All rights reserved. No part of this publication may be reproduced, stored in a retrieval system, or transmitted, in any form or by any means, electronic, mechanical, photocopying, recording, or otherwise without the prior permission in writing of the publisher.

Disclaimer
This is a work of fiction. Names, characters, businesses, places, events and incidents are either the products of the author's imagination or used in a fictitious manner. Any resemblance to actual persons, living or dead, or actual events is purely coincidental. In no way do I or the publisher recommend trying any of the methods put forward in this book. It is purely and solely for entertainment purposes.

ISBN-10: 0986117404
ISBN-13: 978-0-9861174-0-4

First published by Lost Sailor Book Press
Sedona Arizona

www.douglaseagen.com

Table Of Contents

Introduction 1

What A Booger Can Do Part 1 5

   The Fact of The Matter Is 11

What A Booger Can Do Part 2 15

   Booger Jokes 21

What A Booger Can Do Part 3 25

   Around The World With Fifteen Boogers 31

What A Booger Can Do Part 4 33

   Once Upon A Booger 39

What A Booger Can Do Part 5 45

Conclusion 51

INTRODUCTION

In the beginning there was the booger. Love em or not, they're here to stay.

Our good friends over at Webster's dictionary define a Booger as: A piece of dried nasal mucus. What! That's it! Now just hold on one booger picking minute!

You, me and every other person that has ever lived on this planet knows that a booger goes far beyond a six word description. I mean come on, six lousy words! I for one think it deserves a better write up than that? Don't you?

Let me tell you. I was frothing and steaming. My fists shook towards the sky. Six lousy words! This book is going to take you far beyond just a description. By the end you'll have a whole new appreciation for our little buddy the booger.

So let me tell you how I got started. I woke up one morning with a stuffy nose. It was so bad I could hardly breathe. I looked in vain for some tissue. No luck. I ran to the bathroom. The toilet paper roll was looking thin. I thought it best to save it for it's intended use.

I went to the porch and tried the old trucker blow. No Luck. This onslaught of nasal mucous meant business. Then it dawned on me. Why not just use my finger? I did it all the time when I was a kid.

I closed the door and got to work. I thought it would be easy. But this was no ordinary booger invasion. Nope this one would take time, technique, and effort.

I brushed away the outside crumbs that had dribbled out and dried onto the skin just below my nostrils. Then I did it. I poked my forefinger up my nostril and started digging around. Once the hard crusty layer was pierced, the gooey, warm, sticky snot was easy to get to.

It flowed out over my fingers and my original dilemma came back to haunt me. No tissue. I looked to my dog sleeping in the corner. Nah, that's not fair. Besides if PETA found out they'd string me up by the nose hairs.

I could just let it dry and then roll it into balls and flick it away. So much was running out of my nose by now I couldn't keep up with it. Soon it covered two fingers, then three!

There has got to be something I can do with all these boogers. I looked around, and then the light bulb went on. Why discard them? There has got to be something I can do with them. I started seeing dozens of uses for them right here in my own home.

My excitement was building as I raced around the house. Soon enough I had compiled a pretty good list. Now my mind, and my nose were really running on overdrive. The more I thought about it, the more it became evident. I could solve a lot of my problems with the use of boogers! And if it worked for me, it can work for others, too. Right?

The past, present, and future all collided. This could be endless. What else could we use boogers for? Heat shields for the space shuttle? A new sustainable supply of clean energy? Im sure glad Humpty Dumpty's men didn't think of this first. Those boys missed the boat. Nope, this idea was mine! Finally, I could leave my mark!

I began listing everything I could think of. And let me tell you, that list could fill volumes. But I can't give away all of my secrets at once, so I've pared it down to a hundred and one. So without further ado and fanfare I introduce to you, (Drum roll please), 101 Things To Do With A Booger

So sit back. Grab a box of tissues and explore the many astounding uses set forth in this book. Pick your favorites and share them with your neighbors, friends, families, and coworkers.

Sincerely,

Han Kerchief

WHAT A BOOGER CAN DO PART 1

1. Fix a flat tire:
Long way from home with no spare and no garage in sight? No problem just take a deep breath and put your nose to the rubber. Blowouts may require several applications.

2. Baby Sitter:
Do your kids keep crawling out of their crib at night? No problem. Right before bedtime attach a booger to the bottom of their diaper and lay them down. They may cry a bit. But they aren't going anywhere!

3. Hang art work on the wall:
Why leave an unsightly nail hole in the wall when the adhesive power of a booger will do. I wouldn't trust my Picasso with this one. But hey, if you're reading this book you probably don't own a Picasso.

4. Repair broken china:
To repair: Blow a booger on both edges of the broken surfaces. Use a q-tip to spread evenly along the cracks. Place the plate in a sunny spot. Allow ample time for drying. Disclaimer: May not be hold up in the dishwasher.

5. Thwart a robbery:
Next time you hear "Stick 'em up buster!" Calmly

pull your money out of your wallet, blow a booger on it and offer it to the would be robber. For extra affect, you can reach around in your butt crack and tell them you think you have spare change also!

6. Fix a squeaky door:
Remove door from its hinges. Apply boogers to all surfaces, including the door jam. This works particularly well during cold and flu season. Warning: This job may not be suitable for all boogers.

7. Use as a clasp on a coin purse:
Do you keep finding change in the bottom of your bag? Close purse, apply booger. It doubles as a rainy day fund, as most merchants won't except your payment. Who knew their was a fortune to be made with a booger!

8. Moisten dog food:
Blow into Fido's favorite bowl. Mix in his favorite dog food and *bon apetit*. " Ew!" you say. "Thats just gross Han." Don't you worry Your dog will love it. After all, he does lick his own butt.

9. Rebind an old book:
Don't let that old Dickens or Hawthorne lose it's pages. You can still treasure these classics for years

to come. It does take some time and a steady hand though. It'll give a new excitement to Moby Dick when Feddalah cries out "Thar she blows!"

10. Bandage substitute:
Cuts can happen anywhere, not just at home. But when was the last time you took a first aid kit to the beach or shopping mall. No kit, no problem. Blow a bit into your palm and rub thoroughly over affected area.

11. Fix a hole in a muffler:
My neighbor Joe gave me the idea for this one. He warms his old dilapidated station wagon up at 6:30 every morning. Rumbles the whole damn house. Blow a nice juicy wad onto a putty knife and patch the hole. Your car will be sounding better in no time.

12. Roll them up and play marbles:
You ever seen a round booger? This one is a great project for kids on a rainy day, as it will take some time. Blow, roll and set by the fireplace to dry. Once their ready you'll be able to knuckle down with the best of the aggies!

13. Seal a drafty window:
Take a bite out of your energy bills. Apply a stream

of boogers along the window pane. It will create an impenetrable barrier, keeping old man winter on his side of the glass. Not recommended if you will be opening and closing often.

14. Keep deck furniture from sliding on a boat:
Got a yacht on the high seas? Here is a great way to keep that lounge chair firmly anchored to the deck . Place a booger on the bottom of each chair leg and hold firmly to the floor. After half an hour it aint going nowhere.

15. Send to your congressman:
"I do solemnly swear to...." Yeah, yeah, yeah. We've all heard that one before. My father used to tell me. If you don't like something, write your congressman. Ha-ha. I've got a better use for that envelope.

16. Stuff a Turkey:
Everybody loves stuffing. And everybody and their mother has the long loved family recipe with it's secret ingredient that has been passed down for generations. Imagine your glee when they ask you how you get it to stay so moist!

17. Remove lint from your belly button:
If you've got an innie, then you've got lint. Before

slapping on that bikini or speedo make sure you wont be embarrassed by a fuzzy navel. Apply a booger to the end of a q-tip and swish. Don't forget your sunblock.

18. Seal an envelope:
Why lick when you can blow? While this hasn't been approved by the post office yet, it hasn't come up on their hazardous materials list either. Through rain or sleet, or even snow, the boogie will keep your contents safe.

19. Put a stamp on a package:
See number 18

20. Thwart an alien invasion:
We've been searching for signs of intelligent life in the universe for decades. Lets show them there is none here. Transmit this book into outer space wavelengths. Those pesky invasion forces will turn around in no time.

The Fact of The Matter Is

I knew my liberal arts college degree would come in handy someday. During my time in school, I wasn't the smartest, the brightest, or the best. But I did learn how to do research.

Lucky for you I've scoured the universe as we know it for facts and figures about our good friend, the booger. I've taken the time to add these facts for those of you who are more scholarly or just enjoy knowing a thing or two about a thing or two!

* What exactly is a booger?

Technically speaking a booger is that slimy gooey stuff known in the scientific or doctorly world as mucus. Mucus membranes line the inside of your nose and secrete snot. And it's that very snot that wards off and protects your airway from invaders such as germs, dust, and pollen. Good thing it cant repel my trusty finger or I'd be out of a good job!

* A boogie from a sneeze can travel up to one hundred miles per hour. Thats about as fast as a cheetah can chase it's prey!

* Your sinuses can make up to two and a half liters of snot per day. Thats like two thirds of a gallon in dog years!

* The world's longest human booger on record is said to be seventeen inches. Holy cow snot!

* The world's longest booger blow in an amazing nineteen and a half feet. And it was blown by a woman! She blew it so far it stuck to the wall across the bar.

* The proper term for picking your nose is Rhinotillexomania. I bet you didn't get that one right at the spelling bee.

* A man in Australia claims to have a booger collection the size of a soccer ball. Hey mate, fancy a game of football? Okay you play goalie!

* It's not only kids who pick their nose. Studies show that 95% of adult pick there nose also. Pick John pick. See John pick.

Scientific studies are now showing that eating your boogers can be beneficial to your health. Thats right. It seems that eating boogers may actually boost your immune system.

* There are about 50 calories in a cup of boogers. Thats about the same amount as a medium bowl of oatmeal. Got a cold? Late for work? You got it. Breakfast on the go!

WHAT A BOOGER CAN DO PART 2

21. Use as bait for fishing:
No worms? No Problem. Apply a nice slimy booger liberally to your hook and you'll be hauling them into your boat in no time! Don't let the hook get too close to your face though. You'll never live it down when you get back to the dock.

22. Fire starter:
It always seems to rain when I go camping, and it's almost impossible to get those soaking logs started. I've found a solution. Mix a booger with a little rubbing alcohol, and apply generously to the logs. You'll be toasting marshmallows in no time.

23. Use as a salve for blisters and cuts:
Clean the affected area thoroughly with soap and water. Grease your palm with a good sneeze, and apply to the affected area. Rinse and repeat for two to three days and you will be good as new.

24. Alternative food source:
Late for work or school? Do you just need a midday snack or pick me up? Put your ego to the side, and just do it. No need for seasoning. Travels wherever you do, and you don't even need to put in a bag.

25. Extra cushion for shoes:
Got an uncomfortable corn or an overworked bunion. Simply line the inside of your shoe with a nice juicy lougey and feel your pain melt away. Works especially well with leather. Ladies, please no open toe shoes for this one.

26. Leather conditioner:
Mix two parts boogers (nice juicy ones) one part lemon juice, and one part olive oil in a blender. Spread liberally with a soft cloth and wipe down to protect your favorite couch, car seat, or expensive jacket.

27. Emergency ear plugs:
Sirens, rock concerts, and jack hammers can do serious damage do your hearing. A little too loud a the club tonight? A good booger can help you keep your hearing intact for years to come. Just don't let the opposite sex whisper sweet nothings!

28. Secret weapon for Jenga champions:
Championship matches can be stressful. And when the pressure is on, you need an edge. Hide a few boogers up your sleeve for those tough maneuvers. "But Han, that would be cheating." I checked the rule book. Boogers aren't even mentioned.

29. Loosen tough bolts:
My mechanic is pissed. He makes a lot of money on stripped bolts that wont come off. My solution saves you time and money. You'll need a real wet one for this. Blow onto stuck bolt and let it sit for an hour. Should come right off.

30. Fix handle on coffee mug:
I accidentally broke mom's favorite mug from Bora Bora while she was in the bathroom. I just knew she'd be heartbroken, and call me a clumsy oaf. I cant handle rejection like that. Yup, you got it, Boogers saved my sanity.

31. Sculpting material:
Have you seen the price of alabaster or marble these days? I swear if it was like this in the old days Michelangelo's, *David* would have been a skinny little pip squeak. Yes indeed, boogers are quickly becoming the hottest new medium to work with!

32. Stops fidgety fingers:
My wife and daughter hate this one. But my six year old son loves it! Apply liberally between each finger and allow to dry. It doubles as a sure fire way to keep your kids from dropping their sippy, or pacifier on the ground.

33. Sooth an upset stomach:

Another, "Ew, Han your disgusting!" I'd tell you, it's more natural approach and twice as effective then that pink stuff you guzzle into your gullet. Tilt your head back and let them slide down the back of your throat. You'll feel better in no time.

34. Fix broken stems on plants:

Take a drinking straw, lube the inside of it with boogies, place over broken stem and slide other end in. Photosynthesis will take over and your tulips, mums and begonias will be blooming in no time.

35. Thicken soups and gravy:

Ah, another culinary secret revealed. I don't think we will see boogers being used as the secret ingredient on any of the new fangled chef shows any time soon. But hey, they use pig jowls, and eel intestines. Boogers might not be so far away after all.

36. Use as fertilizer:

Lets face it. It is time to rid our soil of those harmful chemicals. For a more natural approach, till a few boogies into your soil. Too grossed- out over this one? Come on, boogers are the new manure. You'll have bumper crops in no time.

37. Replacement for worn cabinet clasps:
Ah the booger once again makes it's appearance for the handyman special. Mold two boogers together. (one dry, and one wet work well in this situation) Cut them in half and apply to door and frame of the cabinet.

38. Sound- proof a room:
This one came in handy after our son came home from school with a trumpet. Apply liberally to the inside of walls. This one took a team effort though. It gave a whole new meaning to family bonding.

39. Cook fries with them:
I bet you never knew that boogers have a high tolerance for heat. Yep just like lard, simply heat up a pan full of boogers and drop your fries in. They'll cook up to a nice golden brown. No need for seasoning!

40. Furniture polish:
Forget those spray cans of chemical soup. A more natural recipe lies in your kitchen and up your nose. Mix a nice long boogie with a little lemon juice and olive oil for a lasting shine that will stick around for a long, long time.

Booger Jokes

* What's the difference between boogers and broccoli?

Kids don't eat broccoli!

* How do you make a tissue dance?

Put a little boogie in it!

* What's the difference between a plate and a booger?

A plate goes on top of the table. A booger goes underneath!

* What's the difference between a prince and a booger?

A prince is the heir to the throne. A booger gets thrown in the air!

* Why did the booger cross the road?

Because the kids were picking on him!

* What do you call a skinny booger?

Slim Pickens!

* What's the stuff that comes out of your dogs nose?

Puppy Chow!

* Knock knock.

Who's there?

Booger snot.

Booger's not here, come back later!

* What do you call a booger that gets caught in your mustache?

A good catch!

* Why don't elephants pick their nose?

There is nowhere to wipe a six foot booger!

WHAT A BOOGER CAN DO PART 3

41. Keep those pesky salesmen away:
Blow a few nice long drippy boogers on your door bell. They'll high tale their vacuums and dictionaries right on down the road. You may miss out on the girl scout cookies though.

42. Write in candidate for president:
Tired of the current political situation. The cold mornings in November are the perfect time for a drippy nose. Slap a boogie on the ballot. No hanging chads with this one. You're vote will be loud and clear. Worse case scenario: is theres a run off!

43. Children's toys:
Have you been to the department store lately? Kids' toys are getting expensive! And most of them are cheap plastic junk. Let's face it, they're are going to play with boogers anyway. What a great way to turn those sick days into play days.

44. Mustache wax:
This is one of my personal favorites. I always wondered how guys got those handlebar mustaches to stand up like that. Until one day, I let my mustache grow, and gave a blow. A little twist at the ends and let it dry. Stayed up for days.

45. Hair mousse:
Punk rockers really love this one. Lather up your hands and spike your hair in no time. Need a little color in that spike. Dig a little deeper until your nose bleeds. A great tip for girls or guys on the go.

46. Emergency shaving cream.
I know, soap works well. But when you add a little boogie your razor will just glide across your face. Works great for frequent fliers. With all of the TSA regulations these days, why fight it?

47. Fix leaky pipes:
Plumber busy? All the benefits without the butt crack! It's hard getting a plumber when you really need one. Don't risk costly damage from a leaky pipe. With fast action and the help of a booger you can save hundreds of dollars.

48. Stabilizer for nuclear meltdowns:
I haven't personally tested this one. But hey why not give it a try? My hypothesis is a deep impenetrable layer of snot might just keep them overheated fuel rods from melting down. Nothing else seems to work. Another great group project.

49. Water sealant:

Has rainy season caught you off guard? Think of all the uses. A natural moisture repellent guaranteed to work every time. Don't believe me? Try it for yourself. Put a boogie in your palm and hold it under a faucet. It repels like magic.

50. Non lethal bullets:

For a kinder gentler nation. Riots and demonstrations are popping up at an alarming rate. Police may be a little quick on the trigger. I say if your gonna shoot, use a boogie as ammo. By time they wipe it off their face, you can have them in cuffs.

51. Wear as a disguise:

A little imagination can go a long way here. Anything from a witches nose, to buck teeth can be molded, and applied with a booger. Personally I like mixing with a little rouge to simulate a gaping zombie head wound.

52. Patch holes in socks:

Everyone has their favorite par of socks they just can't bear to get rid of. We will wear them until our feet blister. I've found a solution. Mix a boogie with that belly button lint we talked abut earlier and patch them holes right up.

53. Fix runs in nylons:
Apply booger to the start of the run. Stops them dead in their tracks. On a side note: Do you know how you can tell if a woman is wearing pantyhose? When she farts her ankles bulge out!

54. Fix worn shoes:
When was the last time you found a cobbler working in America? No not a peach or a cherry, silly. A cobbler used to be an integral part of society, fixing shoes and boots. Slap a piece of leather and a boogie on the offending hole, and hi ho, hi ho, it's off to work you go.

55. Spitball adhesive:
I mean hey if your gonna launch a spitball at someone, you might as well make it stick. I suggest the jumbo straws. Cocktail straws, and bendy's need not apply!

56. Throat lozenge:
Just tilt your head back and feel the relief. If you want it to have that same sweet taste as the store bought ones, have drink a glass of cherry juice and swish it in with the booger. Works every time.

57. Dip for chips:
I know this one is just totally gross, but somehow

you knew it was coming! Tired of dip that slides right off the chip? Chop a little onion, tomato and peppers and you have fresh salsa that is guaranteed to stick to any chip.

58. Mix with your favorite drinks:
Run out of bitters? No problem! "I'll have a martini with boogers please. Oh and uh, pass the chips."

59. Emergency suture or stitch:
I was out fishing one day and fell and cut my arm open. The cut was pretty deep, but the fish were still biting. I looked towards the car, and thought about the hospital. Luckily just then I had to sneeze. I held my arm out, and blew. The cut was sealed!

60. Skin conditioner:
Eyelids a little saggy? Double chin got you down. Forget those expensive spa treatments. Slide a boogie over the offending sag or blemish. Let sit for a couple hours and rinse. You'll be amazed at the results.

AROUND THE WORLD WITH FIFTEEN BOOGERS

Everybody, I mean everybody from all around the world has boogers. Wouldn't it be nice to know how to say booger in another language? I thought so. I sent my crack team of booger reporters and scholars to the far and near reaches of the world to gather this information. After we compiled the data I asked them to pick a few of their favorites.

* Arabic – *Wasax al-anf*

* Belarutian – *Kazjauka*

* Chinese – *Bishi*

* Czech – *Sopel*

* Danish – *Bussemand*

* Estonian – *Koll, Konn*

* French – *Cotte de nez*

* German – *Popel*

* Italian – *Caccola*

* Japanese – *Hanakuso*

* Norwegian – *Buso*

* Polish – *Koza*

* Romanian – *Muc*

* Spanish – *Moco*

* Turkish – *Sumuk*

WHAT A BOOGER CAN DO PART 4

61. Toothpaste:
Have you ever had a cavity in your nose? I didn't think so. Squeeze a little boogie onto the bristles and brush back and forth with vigor. Works wonders for your gum line too!

62. Fills crack in plaster walls:
I recently visited a friend in San Francisco. The walls in his house cracked time and time again from all the earthquakes. "Han, it's hard to find someone to fix them." I just smiled and got to work!

63. Use as bait in a mousetrap:
Have you seen the price of cheese lately? And them damn mice are getting picky. American, or swiss just doesn't seem to do the trick anymore. Use extreme caution when loading the trap. The first time I tried it I almost lost my nose!

64. Notary seals:
Save the wax for candles and use a booger. It also gives your important documents their own special DNA signature.

65. Steel strengthener:
Fire them old foundries back up and let's put America back to work. I can see it now: Boogers the new

natural resource. Works especially well with steel cables that need a little flexibility.

66. Repair broken eyeglass frames:
Come on, tape just makes you look stupid.

67. Bookmark:
Just make sure it is a page you have already read.

68. Insect repellant:
Avoid those nasty chemicals and lather up with a boogie. It creates an impenetrable barrier that'll break the mouths right off those pesky little buggers. Also repels mothers in law!

69. Newscaster for local TV station:
These guys all look and talk the same anyway. The ratings would go through the roof. "Now reporting live from the scene of the accident. "Booger, what can you tell us?" "Well Dan, its a real sticky situation we have down here."

70. Dreadlock starter kit:
Wanna look cool or hip, (or just piss off your parents), but your hair is to thin for dreadlocks? That's right, a booger can help with that. Apply liberally and start twisting. *Ja man*!

71. Adhesive for fly strip:
Yep, attract them and keep them. Even the extra strong horse flies can't get away from the powerful adhesive qualities of a boogie.

72. Trade on the stock market:
I ran this idea by my broker. He thought it was terrific! "Heck Han, a lot of stocks out there have no value anyway." Commodities may never be the same.

73. Fill sandbags for flood walls:
The problem with most sandbags is they are filled with sand. You ever see what happens to sand when water hits it. Yeah it turns to mud and washes away. This won't happen to a boogie. Another great team building exercise.

74. Repair potholes:
A great idea to cut down on Municipal budgets. Team up with the hospital during flu season for maximum savings. The more uses I find the more sense #72 makes. Buy early folks. You can make a fortune.

75. Break up a fist fight:
The old fashioned way of jumping in between two or more fighters just gets you hurt. I have a new idea. Run up holding for a boy blow and yell, "I'll snot

ya!" Watch the combatants flee.

76. Alternative fuel for mass transit:
You've heard of bio-diesel. How about boogie-diesel? The sustainable, and virtually pollution free alternative to fossil fuel.

77. Pay my mortgage:
Through the sale of this book!!

78. Soften sharp corners:
If you've got kids you know how often they bump into the sharp corners of cabinets, tables, and chairs. Smooth out sharp corners on furniture to avoid injury and costly doctor bills.

79. Ski wax:
Directions: Blow on the bottom of your boards, and run a nice hot iron over it. You'll be shushing down that hill faster than you ever have. Works well on snowboards too.

80. Candle fuel:
Fill a small glass with boogers. Tamp down until it's nice and smooth on the top. Add a wick, and light! Add vanilla or any other scent that floats your boat. Hmm, speaking of floating your boat! I just came up with another use!

Once Upon A Booger

Once upon a time:

There was an old crusty booger that lived up nostril hill
He brewed up the phlegm balls that made people ill.

One night he was tired and left the booger still on high
He woke in the morning too so many boogers, they covered the sky.

He told them to get lost, he was getting real mad
They doubled, then tripled, it was getting quite bad.

They told them they were staying at least for a day
There was nothing he could do to get them out of the way.

He called his friend finger, that lived outside of his world
He begged him to come in and give em a twirl.

Finger he came, and twirl yes he did
And wouldn't you know it, them boogers they slid.

Down nostril hill, and out into the light.
Joe thought he was done, and went to bed for the night.

The very next day they were back again.
Joe got on the phone and called up a friend.

Sneeze my old pal, Im in need of some help
Sneeze jumped on his hanky and let out a yelp.

Booger my old friend I'd be happy indeed
To help you out of this trouble, with whatever you need.

So he reared back and sniffled the boogers caught in the nose hairs
He jumped and he bellowed and shot them out in the air.

Well soon old Joe's pleasure had turned into fright
He'd been plucked from the nostril, and been thrown out of sight.

He flew through the air and stuck to the side of a tree
He got buzzed and poked by a big bumble bee.

The bee flew him home and they entered the hive
After a harrowing flight Joe was happy to just be alive.

Then later a man came and scooped out the honey
Put it in a glass jar and sold it for money.

Joe felt at home in this soft sticky mess
And along came a girl in a little pink dress.

She took home the honey and spread it on bread
And down the gullet he went, Joe thought he was dead!

He swam and he floated and he stuck to a rib bone
He though this is not bad I think ill call it my home.

The girl she grew up and became a big star
She had her own airplane, a mansion, and a big fancy car.

Old Joe the booger he traveled the world
Till the day she got sick and her stomach it hurled.

Joe hit the sidewalk and stuck to the side of wall
Till a dog sniffed and licked him down, one gulp and all.

They frolicked and ran and played in the water
And one day the dog had six sons and two daughters.

Now Joe was as proud as any booger could be
Like a proud booger papa it was good to be free.

From the hassles and late nights of running a still
That made up the phlegm balls that made people ill.

It is much better living with puppies and dogs
rolling in mud puddles and jumping on logs.

Truth be it told, he never liked his old job
He was just stuck, like an old dried up blob.

There's one thing I think every booger should know
If you are felling stuck, Just give it a blow!

So the moral of the story should be easy to see.
Get out of your own way, get unstuck, and be free.

The End

WHAT A BOOGER CAN DO PART 5

81. Gym buddy:
Do you ever go to the gym, and everyone tries to poach your barbell right in the middle of your set? No respect! A good blow and wipe on the bar will keep even the most burly of he-men away!

82. Rave necessity:
Everybody knows that raves can go on for hours and sometimes last all night. Do you really want to sweat off that last bit of glitter or extra long fake eyelash before the last ecstatic DJ finishes their show? Look no further than your friendly booger.

83. Build a ginger bread house:
I know you've been wondering how the heck they get those walls and ceilings to stay put without nails, or glue. Yep, another secret revealed. Unfortunately, boogers don't work that well for sandcastles.

84. Remote control locator:
In this day and age who has time to look for remote control to the TV? Just stick a booger on it and attach it to the arm of your chair. I guarantee your teenagers wont be using your TV for video games!

85. Refrigerator magnet:
Another handy tool from the chef's bag. Twice as

strong for a fraction of the price of ordinary kitchen magnets.

86. Appetite suppressant:
Don't ruin your dinner with that late afternoon sandwich or candy bar. Try a boogie, that should hold you over. It works especially well if you give it a good long look before choking it down.

87. Table coaster:
Nobody likes those offending water stains on their furniture. Nice soft boogies work best for this. Place on the bottom of the glass and problem solved. Warning: Do not let sit overnight.

88. Hand warmer:
You've never picked out a cold one, have you? Just blow a big sneeze directly into your palms and rub vigorously. They'll be warmed up in no time!

89. Chewing gum replacement:
No need to head to your local convenience store when you've got a boogie just waiting to be chewed. Hey, as long as you don't swallow you can chew away. Long lasting flavor. Not recommended for blowing bubbles.

90. Fix a broken heel:

A great one for the ladies. Have you ever been tearing it up on the dance floor, and your heel busts off? Not to worry. Just head to the nearest powder room and goob on a boogie. You'll be dancing the night away in no time!

91. Fuel for bad jokes:

See chapter three

92. Tendon replacement:

Medical research has shown that a booger is pliable enough to stretch, and strong enough not to break. Also great for cartilage replacement. These methods are still in the experimental stages.

93. Driveway sealant:

Don't let the wear and tear of everyday use and weather ruin your driveway. Get the family together for a sealing day. Heck, make a weekend out of it. Invite your friends over. Have a cook out. Look out, Uncle Bob is going in for more!

94. Vitamin supplement:

They say your body can heal itself with good nutrition. I say all the extra nutrients and minerals are locked up there in your schnozz. Warning: As of publishing this has not been approved by the FDA.

95. Fashion tool:
Need a quick lace border around that new pair of jeans? Want to attach rhinestones to your favorite jacket? Need it in a hurry? Don't waste precious ME time with a needle and thread. Try a boogie and get out their and show off!

96. Barter for goods and services:
Any takers out there? I'll trade you a nose full if you'll cut my lawn.

97. Prop open windows on a warm night:
Nothing bothers me more than my window slamming shut and waking me up on a hot summer night. Place a booger between the top of the window, and the frame. Hold in place for about five seconds and let the crickets chirp you to sleep.

98. Survival tool:
There are way too many applications to list here. The last ninety seven are a good start though.

99. Flick at your brother or sister:
If you didn't do this as a kid I know you at least thought about it. When they are not looking dig in

and roll up between thumb and forefinger. Even if you miss you'll be smiling away.

100. Hand cleaner:
Just blow and wipe. Takes off the toughest dirt and grime. not recommended for food service workers.

And finally!! Drum roll please.

101. Emergency birthday present
For that special someone that seems to have everything. Just put a bow on a boogie and attach it to a copy of this book. Sure to please even the pickiest (pun intended) friend or family member!

CONCLUSION

So there you have it. All the things you ever wanted to know about boogers. And quite a few you probably didn't.

As you can see, a booger is indeed, more than simply a booger. I'm glad I had the chance to open your eyes to this new and fascinating world. I'm not sure if you want to thank me, or flick one at me! Either way, thanks for reading this book. I'm sure part of the proceeds will go towards a new box of tissue.

We covered a lot of ground. Fact, fiction, tools, jokes, translations, heck we even threw in a little philosophy. Now it is up to you to come up with your own useful, or not so useful things to do with a booger.

Stay tuned for other books from this author. Heck, go to his website. His alter ego spins a pretty good tale himself. Blogs, books, and more. A little different from the critical acclaim he's seeking from humor, but nonetheless a fine writer.

You can reach him at, www.douglaseagen.com

From the bottom of my heart, to the top of my nose,
I wish you a fine day!

Han Kerchief

www.ingramcontent.com/pod-product-compliance
Lightning Source LLC
Chambersburg PA
CBHW041811040426
42450CB00001B/2